Luba, Simply Luba

Luba, Simply Luba

Diane Flacks
Luba Goy
Andrey Tarasiuk

Luba, Simply Luba
first published 2013 by
Scirocco Drama
An imprint of J. Gordon Shillingford Publishing Inc.
© 2013 Written by Diane Flacks in collaboration with Luba Goy and Andrey Tarasiuk
Reprinted February 2014.

Scirocco Drama Editor: Glenda MacFarlane
Cover design by Terry Gallagher/Doowah Design Inc.
Cover photo by Richard Picton
Ms. Goy's vinok created by Natalka Husar
Photo of Diane Flacks by Helen Tansey
Photo of Luba Goy by Russ Martin
Photo of Andrey Tarasiuk by Joy von Tiedemann

Printed and bound in Canada on 100% post-consumer recycled paper.

We acknowledge the financial support of the Manitoba Arts Council and The Canada Council for the Arts for our publishing program.

Library and Archives Canada Cataloguing in Publication

Flacks, Diane, author
    Luba, simply Luba / by Diane Flacks in collaboration with Luba Goy and Andrey Tarasiuk.

ISBN 978-1-897289-97-6 (pbk.)

    1. Goy, Luba--Drama. I. Goy, Luba, author
II. Tarasiuk, Andrey, author III. Title.

PS8561.L264L83 2013   C812'.6   C2013-906552-0

J. Gordon Shillingford Publishing
P.O. Box 86, RPO Corydon Avenue, Winnipeg, MB Canada R3M 3S3

Acknowledgements

It takes many people and organisations to help create, develop and produce a new play. We would like to thank Red Boots Canada for commissioning and developing the play and Red Boots Canada and Pleiades Theatre for producing the play in Toronto. Thanks also to the BCU Foundation, Metcalf Foundation, Ontario Arts Council, Shevchenko Foundation, St. Vladimir Institute, The Temerty Family Foundation and the Toronto Arts Council for their assistance in the writing, development and producing of the play.

Thanks must go to the following individuals for their inspiration, support, help and commitment to the project: Suzanne Bolton and Jeff Mooney, Ron Chyczij, Sandra Faire and Ivan Fecan, Don Ferguson, Mimi Goyer, Natalka Husar, Christine Kuzyk, John D. McKellar, John A. Miller, Richard Picton, Dorothy Post, Timothy and Frances Price, Peter Riddihough, Senator Nancy Ruth, John Van Burek and Cylla von Tiedemann.

Production History

Luba, Simply Luba premiered on May 9, 2012 at the Berkeley Street Theatre, Downstairs, Toronto, ON. It was produced by Red Boots Canada in association with Pleiades Theatre with the following cast and artistic team:

LUBA...Luba Goy

BANDURIST / BASS..Victor Mishalow

Directed by Andrey Tarasiuk

Set Design by Douglas Paraschuk

Costume Design by Tamara Marie Kucheran

Lighting Design by Raha Javanfar and Robert Thomson

Props Master: David Hoekstra

Music Director: Victor Mishalow

Stage Manager: Bill Jamieson

Luba, Simply Luba was the first work commissioned and developed by Red Boots Canada. Led by Andrey Tarasiuk, the company takes its name and its logo / symbol from the choboty which all young people of Ukrainian heritage have worn as members of local dancing troupes, in Andrey's case as a founding member of Winnipeg's renowned Rusalka Ukrainian Dance Ensemble.

Red Boots would like to acknowledge the partnership opportunity which Pleiades Theatre and its Founder / Artistic Director, John Van Burek, extended for the initial run in Toronto.

Production Note: Italicized text in stage character exchanges indicates that particular character speaking in Ukrainian or in a Ukrainian accent.

Diane Flacks

...is a writer/performer in theatre, radio and television. She has been lauded for her four critically acclaimed solo shows that she wrote and performed in beginning with—*Myth Me, By a Thread, Random Acts*, and *Bear With Me*—and her Floyd S. Chalmers Play Award nominated collaborations with Richard Greenblatt: *Sibs* and *Care*, produced at the Tarragon Theatre.

Diane has also written for, and appeared on, numerous Canadian television series, including *The Kids in the Hall*, for which she was nominated for a writing Emmy, and *The Broadside, Listen Missy* and *PR*—all of which she co-created, co-wrote and acted in.

She has been a feature columnist for the *Toronto Star* and *The Globe and Mail* and can be heard in your car as CBC Radio's national parenting columnist, and as a regular contributor to *Definitely Not the Opera*. Her book, *Bear With Me, What They Don't Tell You About Pregnancy and New Motherhood* was published by McClelland & Stewart.

Ms. Flacks, a mother of two boys, is very happy to be out of the house.

Luba Goy

…is an orginal member of Canada's most popular and enduring comedy troupe, the Royal Canadian Air Farce, and is one of this nation's most beloved comedic actors.

She is a graduate of the National Theatre School of Canada and is immensely proud of her Ukrainian heritage. Luba began her professional career with the Stratford Festival Theatre, and was honoured to return there in the summer of 2002 where she starred in *The Fellini Radio Plays* by Federico Fellini. Her other work includes numerous commercials, roles in film including *Vidma*, a feature shot in Kyiv, Ukraine and voice-over work in animated series.

Ms. Goy has won many awards and received countless honours with the Royal Canadian Air Farce, including the Gemini Humanitarian Award, the Governor General's Performing Arts Award, fifteen ACTRA Awards, a Gemini, a Juno and a star on Canada's Walk of Fame.

Luba is also thrilled with the two Honorary Doctorates she has received: "Mama is so proud, she tells everyone Luba barely finished high school, but she's a doctor!".

Andrey Tarasiuk

...is a a graduate of the University of Manitoba and the National Theatre School of Canada, has been associated with almost every major theatre in this country. Currently he is the producer of Toronto's Pleiades Theatre and the founder of Red Boots Canada Inc.

At the Stratford Festival, where he was Associate Artistic Director and Head of New Play Development for eight seasons, Mr. Tarasiuk also directed a number of productions including James Reaney's *The Donnellys: Stick and Stones* which was also presented at the National Arts Centre, Anne Chislett's *Quiet in the Land*, and the premiere of Anton Piatigorsky's *Eternal Hydra*.

He initiated and acted as the founding producer of Toronto's The Dream in High Park, the acclaimed Canadian Stage outdoor Shakespeare production, and the director of many radio dramas with CBC Radio Canada. He has been a guest director and instructor at the National Theatre School of Canada, the University of Winnipeg and the National Arts Centre.

Andrey is the recipient of a number of awards and distinctions including both the Derek F. Mitchell Artistic Director's Award and the Tyrone Guthrie Award from the Stratford Festival.

Lights and music up:

Ukrainian Church Mass in progress.

LUBA, wearing a stylish silk jacket, pants, little white church gloves, a 1950s style church hat with feathers, holding a little purse, enters the house through the audience.

She's a nine-year old girl, late for church, interacting with the audience as she works her way to the stage.

There is a bench in the centre of the stage, underneath a little mini chandelier with a little red light.

Onstage is a musician/singer (BANDURIST/ BASS.). She reaches the stage.

LUBA then moves to centre stage, kneels and crosses herself.

BANDURIST
/BASS: *(Church Mass in progress with specific section sung in Ukrainian.) ...Virhiu...*

She joins in the prayer in Ukrainian; can't find her prayer book. Looks in a little purse for it, finds it, looks for the place in the book.

Interrupts herself blowing feathers off of her church hat and giggling to her friend, Oksana, beside her.

YOUNG
LUBA: Bruck ...buck...buck... *(Giggles.)*

She sings along to Virhiu, now really getting into

> *it. She blows a feather off her face and giggles and*
> *"brucks" some more like a chicken.*

Bruck...bruck...buck...buck

LUBA/BASS: *(Together, sing.) A-a-a-minnn.*

> *She plays this section out as herself and Oksana,*
> *and the PREIST is played out by the BANDURIST/*
> *BASS.*

PRIEST: *Icyc Xpuctoc, prayshov na dnes, shchob spasteh*
luydstvoh... And Jesus Christ came down to this
earth to save human kind.

YOUNG
LUBA: buck...buck...buck

PRIEST: What does that mean...

> *LUBA blows the feather off, and she's laughing and*
> *doing it more and more.*

...that Jesus Christ came down to earth to save
human kind?

YOUNG
LUBA: buck...buck...buck

PRIEST: "Luba...

> *LUBA reacts as herself, caught, making buck buck*
> *noises.*

...we're waiting, have you laid your egg?"

> *LUBA reacts, one last blow of the feather on the*
> *hat.*

YOUNG
LUBA: Brruck?

> *Lights and music transition out of church.*

LUBA: *(As herself, an adult, to audience.).* Sorry. I'm always late. I've always, always been late, even as a little girl. I'm known as Princess Luba Late of the Danforth.

As you know, I am a woman of a certain age. And, probably like many of us here tonight, at a certain crossroads in life.

And at this point, the past and present, they chase each other around in my brain like two squirrels in a blue bin.

I may be in a taxi, heading to see my baby grandson, and suddenly I'm fifteen years old, in Ottawa, "falling in love" with my first gay man and deciding to go into the theatah! Memories just ambush you. And stories need to be told.

But don't worry, I'm not going to burden you with my whole life story or anything, you know, just the good parts.

Well, the important parts, the ones that, at my age, I should really have put behind me by now, *(Starting to ramble in typical LUBA fashion.)* which is hard to do when memories keep jumping around, and frankly, at my age, it's so easy to lose one's thread at the best of times, especially when there is no teleprompter!?— *(She's lost her thread.)*

…where was I?

> *She looks at the BANDURIST/BASS, who sings, as a reminder:*

BASS: *AA-MIN…*

LUBA: Right! Church. Every Sunday. Religiously! I loved church. It was so dramatic, the music, the altar, the hats, the white gloves, little purses, just like the Queen. (Wait for it, I'm not going to— *(Imitates the*

Queen.) "hmm hmm it's a pleasure to be here at the theatre" —No. Not yet.).

> *She blows the feather one more time and removes the hat.*

My father / Tato never allowed me to miss a single Sunday Mass. "You have mumps? Good. Go to church, pray, you'll feel better." He was born Ukrainian Greek Catholic and my mother was Ukrainian Greek Orthodox. The Catholics and Orthodox hated each other, "both worshiping God in their own vicious way."

My parents met and fell in love in the forced-labour camps in Germany during WWII. They were nineteen years old. Now, this is is not "camp", like Kumbaya; but like get-up-at-five-am-and-go-work-in-the-coal-mines kind of camp. The Gestapo could care less whether they were Catholic or Orthodox—they were all Ukrainians: *Untermensch,* the underpeople. To my mother it was all the same: God was God, and Stepan Goy was handsome… My Tato, on the other hand, hated everybody equally: the Bolsheviks, the Commies, the Russians, the Nazis, the Jews, the Baptists, the Poles the Melnikivtsi—who could not agree with the Banderivtsi, and don't get me started on the atheists, but Olya was gorgeous and soon, pregnant. With me.

(To God.) What would my Tato think of me now: divorced, four cats, an actress, impersonating politicians and nuns, pretending to be in a church!, and *(confessionally.)* what *does* it mean that Jesus Christ came down to earth to save human kind?

BANDURIST
/ BASS: *A-a-a-minnn.*

LUBA: Well, I don't know, but as soon as I had a child, I decided not to take any chances with the Big Guy.

I made my son Gabriel go to Ukrainian school and Ukrainian dance and church *every* Sunday, just like I'd had to! The poor thing.

She plays this section out as herself and GABE and the PRIEST.

Gabe took it seriously, just like I did. When he was five, the Priest was saying, "Christ carried the cross." Gabe puts his little five year-old hand up.

GABE: Father Sianchuk?

PRIEST: Yes, Gabriel.

GABE: It must have been heavy. It must have weighed at least as much as a couple of 4X4's.

PRIEST: Ah, Gabriel, I see you're still renovating your house.

LUBA: And I still am. Renovating. My house. *(Indicates her gorgeous self.)*

Lights and music transition into Ottawa home.

LUBA pulls some toy furniture out of the bench.

My house, so to speak. I'm ten years old, living in Ottawa in two rooms on the second floor of a house: living room / dining room / kitchen—no fridge, no sink *(She tosses the toy sink and fridge away.)*—and one bedroom. We shared a bathroom with five other boarders. It was great. There was always someone to talk to!

And the kitchen was always filled with my father's cohorts, and all they did was argue about politics. They'd be sitting around plotting. *Plotke.* My Tato / Stepan's on a rant, with his two compatriots: Mikhailo, the Henchman, and Slavko, the Dandy.

Lighting change.

> *LUBA does a quick imitation of MAMA and these UKRAINIAN HOT HEADS, smoking and plotting. Like the Mafia, they're turning to STEPAN for his opinion.*

STEPAN: *(In Ukrainian.)* ...Hloptsi, oboviaskovo zbydshyvatys proteh tykh Proklyatykh Moskaliv!! Ott shcho! Mikhailo?

MIKHAILO: *(In Ukrainian.)* ...Stepaneh, ta podumaj sobhi cholovicheh nemah orhanizatsiyi! Ott shcho! Slavko?

SLAVKO: *(Holds a tea cup with his pinky up, and delicately dips a cookie in and in Ukrainian.)* ...Pani Olya, pecheh naykraschi honey cookie! Ott shcho!

LUBA: Mama is ironing Tato's shirt...she would take a mouth full of water...then spray it out over the shirt. *(LUBA does the sound of the hot iron hissing.)* She's rolling her eyes.

I'm sitting on the kitchen couch, listening.

STEPAN: To free Ukraine, we must infiltrate the government, from the outside in. We'll storm the Ukrainian Parliament, six or seven of us, maybe ten, if we can get weapons.

MIKHAILO: You want weapons? I can get weapons!

SLAVKO: From where, Mikhailo? Under your bed? *(Laughs.)*

MIKHAILO: *(MIKHAILO gets up to attack him.)* What, you don't believe me?

STEPAN: Mikhailo, Slavko, settle down. What we have that they don't is the element of surprise.

SLAVKO: Surprise? Crazy you. *(Laughs.)*

MIKHAILO: You be shutup! What do you know?

STEPAN: Who's crazy?

LUBA: Mother is rolling her eyes and just keeps ironing.

STEPAN: *(To MAMA.)* I would give up my life for the cause. Every drop of blood for *Ukraina*—

MIKHAILO: Me too! *Dhai Bhozheh!*

SLAVKO: *(Giving in.)* Okay, okay, me too. *Na Zdorovia.*

> *LUBA is still listening and is horrified.*

YOUNG
LUBA: *(As a ten year old.)* Tato! You're going to give up your life? What about Mama and me?

STEPAN: If it wasn't for *you*...

YOUNG
LUBA: Tato!

> *MAMA ironing again*

MAMA: Stepan, that's enough *Plotke*! I'm working all day like a horse in the field, until I'm falling off my feet! And I'm raising Luba! 'free Ukraine from the outside in'? *Znayesh scho...potchelew meni sraku.* Kiss my ass.

> *LUBA reacts as STEPAN is chastised.*

STEPAN: *(To the cohorts.)* Pardon...

LUBA: *(As herself, an adult, to audience.)* So Tato goes to Mama and delicately, kisses her...

> *As she speaks, as STEPAN, she struts, charmingly over to MAMA, goes down on one knee and mimes lifting up her skirt. And, kisses her ass delicately. Then kisses her hand.*

STEPAN: *(To Olya.)* Okay? *(Now he turns to LUBA.)* Dobreh. Luba, you go to school; tell the teacher to write to the Prime Minister to say *Ukraina* needs to be free. You're my messenger, Luba. You.

YOUNG
LUBA: *(As a ten year old.)* But Tato, *slewchai*, I don't want to be your messenger. I just want to be a good Canadian.

STEPAN: Yes, yes, of course, "Good Canadian": hockey, yo-yo, hula-hoop. But then, it's God and *Ukraina*, my little messenger!

             Lights and music. Transition into the woods.

LUBA: I could be a Partisanka, hiding in the forests of *Ukraina* with the other resistance fighters: the Underground; covert cells of strapping young boys and girls together. With machine guns, and uniforms, made-to-measure, with little cute cadet caps, and a sash. Alerting each other to the approach of the enemy with our secret, stealth warning calls.

             Lights change.

             She's in the woods. She imagines being in the woods, hiding, calling signals to other partisans in the woods — she does a tiny bird call, owl, crow, chipmunk, dog, duck, sheep, elephant, wild chimp. Her woods spying goes off the rails...

             Gun shot.

             LUBA acts as if she's been shot.

             Lights restore.

Dammit. I would have been shot on the spot, but they never would have forgotten me.

             Transition into sea voyage.

             LUBA makes the sound of a seagull. A dolphin..

             BANDURIST/BASS does the sound of a big boat.

She pulls a toy boat out of the bench, which she plays with under this speech.

(Unsteadily on her feet with the toy boat.) Whoa-Hospodeh! October 15th, 1951. Sailing to Canada on a big ship *(She uses the boat and acts sea-sick.)* like all the immigrants at that time. Storms! Riding them out strapped to our bunks. We finally arrived at Pier 21 in Halifax *(She acts as if she's getting off the rough boat ride.).*

It's a good thing in those days, the Canadian immigration authorities didn't ask those tough questions.

IMMIGRATION
OFFICIAL: You can come in, you can come in. You, little girl, are you going to make fun of the government when you grow up?

YOUNG
LUBA: Oh yes sir every Friday night at 8 o'clock on CBC.

IMMIGRATION
OFFICIAL: You, back on the boat. Mother, father welcome to Canada—

YOUNG
LUBA: I was just kiddin—

IMMIGRATION
OFFICIAL: Back on the boat—

YOUNG
LUBA: Just kidding—

IMMIGRATION
OFFICIAL: Back on the boat, you little terrorist!

LUBA: I didn't actually talk back to the big immigration fella… In fact, I prayed. I got down on my little knees on the pier and prayed.

YOUNG
LUBA:

Dear Lord, *Bozheh,* please, I ask you for a good life here in Canada for Tato and Mama and me. *Aaminn.* Oh, and, if you can, lots of poppyseed cake. Thank you. And, if it's not too much to ask, a pussy-cat! Two pussy-cats! And a pony! And, *(Looks around to make sure no one is watching.)* let there be no war and no *(Whispered.)* POLITICS!

LUBA:

Yeah, right. How did I end up talking politics on stage, radio and television for thirty five years with the Royal Canadian Air Farce? If it were a life sentence, I would have been out by now.

I went through nine Prime Ministers in my time with Air Farce. Unlike in Tato's Ukraine, we could make fun of our political leaders without being thrown in the Gulag. My Tato would be amazed that we got away with stuff like this:

PIERRE
TRUDEAU:

(She does the rose in the lapel, she raises her middle digit.) Absolutely, I'm bringing in the War Measures Act. Just watch me. Fuddle duddle.

JOE CLARK:

Ho ho ho...I was Canada's most popular Prime Minister for nine whole months. I wasn't in long enough to screw up like the rest of them.

And my favourite,

JEAN
CHRETIEN:

Eh, fer sures don't mess with da little guy from Shawinigan. Or I grabs you by the throat, hit you with my Eskimo sculpture, and my Mounties, dey pepper spray your face—

IMMIGRATION
OFFICIAL:

Okay, that's too much! You can't say that— Back on the boat!

PIERRE
TRUDEAU: You can't put me on the boat, I'm here to stay.

                 She does a pirouette.

                 Lights restore.

LUBA: If my Tato were alive, he would have loved that.
                 He was an actor. In the labour camps in Germany,
                 he had his own theatre! He was a little taller than
                 me, wiry, handsome, with blue eyes, a little Charlie
                 Chaplin mustache, and expressive hands. And that
                 voice! He was a tenor. He played the mandolin; he
                 did stand-up! He could really write the heck out of
                 a joke. Listen to this:

                 *(As STEPAN doing an absurd stand up routine about
                 the war—in Ukrainian gibberish—clownlike—Selepko
                 goes to a café in Paris.)*

                 ...Selepko poyihav do Paruzshy.

                 ...Obsluha putayeh, putayeh yoho..."Qu'est-ce que
                 vous voulez"?

                 ...Selepko kashjeh...Pryhneseh meni KAVY!

                 ...Obsluha putayeh...PARDONNEZ MOI?

                 ...Niii...Tyt PERDYNIV NEMAH!

                 (She mimes a fart.) ...PARDON.

                 Isn't that hilarious? And he was equally good at
                 drama. Tato would act out everything. "Storytime"
                 was always fun at our house.

                 Lights and music. Transition to Ottawa home.

                 My Tato would be sitting on the couch, and I'd be
                 on the floor, leaning on his knee, watching him
                 read from the *Kobzar (Mimes hoisting a massive,
                 heavy book.)* by Taras Shevchenko. A Kobzar is like

a wandering minstrel, or messenger, usually, for some reason, blind. Of course we all loved the stories. Taras Shevchenko is Ukraine's national poet, Ukraine's Robbie Burns. He was imprisoned for his passionate nationalistic poetry for sixteen years in the dungeons in the 1840s, doing forced labour. His manuscript, the *Kobzar*, was smuggled out of the dungeon walls, which is all very tragic and creepy and exciting when you're seven.

Our favourite poem from the *Kobzar* was the story of *Kateryna*.

> *LUBA does STEPAN in Ukrainian, then transitions to English as STEPAN—reciting sections of the poem:*
>
> *...Kochaytusia, chornobrubvi,*
>
> *Ta ne z Moskaljamuh,*
>
> *Bo Moskalji—chuzhji liuduh,*
>
> *Roblyiat lucho z vamheh.*

Once upon a time a very young and beautiful Ukrainian woman, Kateryna, fell in love with a wealthy and powerful Moscovite soldier, who wooed her.

> *...Moskalji lyubut zhartuyuchu,*
>
> *Zhartuyuchu kuneh;*
>
> *Pideh v cvoyu Moskovschchunuh,*
>
> *A divchunah huneh...*
>
>
> *Lights and music transition.*
>
> *She acts this out in a "melodramatic" style as she's*

telling the story and reciting certain passages in Ukrainian, as STEPAN.

LUBA: Her parents warn her to keep away, but she doesn't listen. No, she's out all night in the garden with her Moscovite lover.

Neh sluchalah Kateryna,

Ni bhatkah, ni nenkuh

One thing led to another, and she got knocked up.

As I got older, Tato read me this part more.

STEPAN: *Slewchai.* I know you're getting to like boys.

LUBA: And Kateryna did not listen.

The Moscovite promises to come back for her, but he abandons her. All alone, she has her baby. Her parents are so ashamed—they're being shunned by the whole village. They throw her out of the house. Desperate, she goes to Moscow and finds the soldier on his horse.

Lights and music silent movie style transition.

LUBA does the sound of the horse hooves and acts out the silent-movie-esque pleading.

He ignores her. *(As KATERYNA.)* "You promised to return to me!" She clutches at his stirrup straps, "Remember your son!" He won't look at her or the baby, "Ivan, stay, I'll weep no more!" He spurs the steed on. *(LUBA does the sound of the horse. KATERYNA is devastated.)*

Lights and music silent movie style stops.

STEPAN: Don't go with boys, Luba!

YOUNG
LUBA: *(As a little girl, caught up in it.)* No, no, Tato.

Silent movie style lights and music resumes.

LUBA: Then Kateryna goes insane, and leaves her baby in the road. The baby reaches for her, its tiny fists opening and closing. "Mama, Mama". Kateryna forces herself to turn away from her child, and runs to the river, drops to the wet dirt to pray, "Oh mighty God, receive my soul", and drowns herself.

Eventually, a blind Kobzar finds the boy, takes him in and they beg in the streets.

The acting style becomes more natural, as LUBA gets more overcome by the story.

Years later the Moscovite comes by with his legitimate family. They are rich. They are in their grand carriage. He sees the child, who looks like Kateryna, begging in the streets. He recognizes himself in those hazel eyes and dark brows. For a moment, does it tug at his heart? Does he remember how Kateryna smelled of the wheat in the field, of resistance and yielding? Maybe he does, for he stops his carriage and surveys the Kobzar and the child… His wife takes pity on the beautiful child and asks to give him some coins. But the Moscovite throws the money on the road, and then, yo, leaves the boy in the dust, picking up the kopecks.

Music stops Lights change.

STEPAN: …goodnight, Luba, sweet dreams.

I'm seven, and I ask my father:

YOUNG
LUBA: *(She's a little girl, stunned by the story, and emotional.)* Why Tato? Why did she leave her baby in the road?! Why did she kill herself?

STEPAN: Because he was a Moscovite! Now, stay away from boys!

Oh, I loved that story.

Maybe it was because of Kateryna that I stayed a virgin until I was married! Well, until I was engaged. At eighteen.

Lights and music. Transition into Stratford.

I'm studying at the National Theatre School in Montreal—and my fiancé Ed is at McGill—and now that we're engaged it's time to lose our virginity

We make a plan. We'll have a romantic losing-our-virginity weekend at the Stratford Festival! We'll watch Shakespeare plays all day, and we'll lose our virginity all night!

I say to Ed, 'But I am not going to go to a hotel with you and pretend we're married. They'll know we're not married yet.'

So we went to a campsite. He told his parents he was going to Stratford with his roommate John, and could he borrow a tent and two sleeping bags?

Okay, so you go to the theatre, to a Shakespeare play, and then you lose your virginity, in a tent! How romantic can it not be!

You wake up in the morning and realize you have your period.

I say to my fiancé, you're going to have to buy me a box of Kotex—remember those huge thick pads? Mattresses. Tell them they're for your mother. Poor guy is in the men's room washing out this sleeping bag, with people thinking, 'What the hell, did he kill her in the night?'

Music: LUBA does the sound of the Stratford Festival fanfare.

That evening, we were watching *Richard III*, at

Stratford, feeling so grown up. Yes, yes, he has a hunchback and kills some little kiddies how droll. Now you're a woman; you lost your virginity in a tent; you got your Dubonnet with a slice of lemon on the rocks...

MOTHER-IN-LAW: Edward?

LUBA: I turn around. My future mother-in-law is there with Ed's father and younger sister.

MOTHER-IN-LAW: Our neighbours gave us these tickets to Stratford, so we decided to come... Luba, Edward, how are you finding the campsite?

LUBA: I can't get away with anything—not even losing my virginity! The truth, dammit, it always comes out! "Yes, I lost it. Get me another Dubonnet! Make it a double!"

Music: LUBA does the sound of the Stratford Festival fanfare.

Ed was the love of my life. He totally believed in my talent. In those days, you couldn't just leave your baby boy with your husband and travel the country doing a radio show with a bunch of guys! I said to him once, "If I ever write a book, I'd dedicate it to you because if it wasn't for you I wouldn't be where I am today." He said, "Oh, you'd find a way...

After fifteen years, the marriage went down ...

Pause.

I had a few relationships after my divorce. And the occasional one night stand. *(She catches some cutie's eye in the audience and flirts with them: "What are you doing after the show ...".)* Don't judge me...no one likes to be alone... And I love men. I would date a guy if he wanted to date me. Mind you, you have to take your clothes off and everything...

She smiles at the BANDURIST/BASS flirtatiously, who plays some Ukrainian dance music. She reacts as if she'd forgotten what comes next, then the music helps her recall.

Where was I? Oh yes! *Kateryna!* Hearing my father tell that story kept me a virgin. And the drama of stories like *Kateryna* also made me want to be a performer.

Transition. The music leads LUBA into the Ukrainian dance section.

By the time I was seven, my plan wasn't to be a tragic poet like Taras Shevchenko or a comedian like my father. I was going to be a dancer, like my mother! It's a much better way to meet boys...

Lights change.

Ukrainian music, and the lights isolate LUBA in a dancing pose. She does some intricate dance gestures.

You watch Ukrainian Dance, the girls are splendid. Their little feet are doing millions of intricate steps *(She does them.)* and the audience barely cares... *(She does a listless clap clap clap.)*

Then the guys show up with their red boots and big pants, and go Barumph! *(She does one big kozatskeh step.)* and the audience roars. *(She does a massive clapping.)*

What do you have to do? Give birth on the stage before you get noticed?!

Look, I'm dancing and I had a baby!

AUDIENCE: Is it a boy? Oh pity, it's not a boy. (*Listless clap clap.*)

LUBA: I would have been a wonderful dancer, but my legs are too long, as you see… So I went into comedy. You win, Tato.

              Music sting.

              Even today, Ukrainians all over Canada remember my Tato. They tell me that he was known as the Charlie Chaplin of the German labour camps.

              Transition.

              LUBA does an imitation of Charlie Chaplin working in the German work camp. Maybe she pulls a Chaplin hat out of the bench. He is being funny amid terribly hard labour.

              In Ottawa, well, Tato couldn't work as an actor anymore. But he had to be who he was. Don't we all? So, instead, he became an artistic force in the Ukrainian community. And he loved to entertain my girlfriends with his mandolin.

              She imitates him playing the mandolin and making up ridiculous songs about her friends when they came to visit.

STEPAN: Oh, it's Bessy, she's so messy, She's got long braids tied with ribbons, and a lovely dress-y.

LUBA: It was so embarrassing!

              My friends would say, "Yer Father's so funny!"

YOUNG
LUBA: Yeah, hope he's not home…

              Other kids wished for money, I wished for my Tato

to be normal; to have lived longer. Maybe he would have mellowed with age.

Mind you, if he hadn't have died young, maybe he would have driven me crazy, like he did my mother...

My Tato had two mandolins, which he played every day of his life. My mother just gave them away after he died. I called her on it not long ago. "I don't have anything of Tato's. Why did you give his *mandolinah* away?"

MAMA: Because *you* didn't want to play with them.

LUBA: Ah, so now it's *my* fault.

But later, my mother admitted the real reason she gave them away.

MAMA: After Tato died, I could hear his *mandolinah* playing in the night.

LUBA: If anybody could return from the dead to play the mandolin to drive my mother crazy, it was my Tato.

STEPAN: (*Singing.*) Yes, dear wife, as you know I may be dead. But I can play this mandolin and I crawl into your bed! Hey! la la la la.

MAMA: Oy! Time for the *mandolinah* to go!

LUBA: After failing to play the mandolin, my parents got me an accordion. I'm nine years old. A Castle Fidardo Moriel Sindrini from Italy. 240 baser, ladies and gentlemen, fully-loaded, mother of pearl, very classy, not garish, a gorgeous sound.

> *She sits. She pulls, Mary-Poppins-like, a small, child-sized accordion out of the bench.*

The accordion went from my chin to my ankles. It

was so heavy they had to strap it onto me with a tea-towel.

LUBA struggles with the accordion.

YOUNG
LUBA: Mama!

MAMA: You'll grow into it.

LUBA: As you can see, I did... Well, in a way I did. When I became a teenager, I got these breasts. They got caught in the bellows. I called it the Ouch ouch stage.

She acts out her breasts getting caught as she plays "The Beer Barrel Polka".

YOUNG
LUBA: This is not a sexy instrument! I won't play it! I won't!

I found out later that my mother was paying every week for two years to get that godawful, beautiful accordion. My mother never told me. She never told me a lot of things...

LUBA and the BASS sing the Ukrainian Taras Shevchenko dirge, "Dymyh-Moji," and it plays under the section below.

For those who don't know, here is a brief summary of the tragic history of Ukraine: We were occupied by the Mongols, the Asiatic nomads, the Poles, the Moscovites, the Tartars, the Austro-Hungarians, the Germans, the Icelanders! And the Egyptians, okay maybe not the Egyptians, but they would have if they could have stood the cold and the perogies. Everyone who was anyone in the last thousand years occupied Ukraine and enslaved, starved, oppressed, and slaughtered its people.

And we have the folk songs to prove it.

She puts the accordion away.

LUBA and the BASS sing a few bars of the Ukrainian folk song, "Stepomh." She really belts it out and has to cut herself off. And then…

LUBA: Rough translation: Mothers *do not* send your sons or daughters to war or else you will end up singing this song…in Ukrainian!

After the war, my parents ended up in Belgium, working in the coal mines, as did many Ukrainians. The Belgians took in the *Dheipysteh*, the displaced people, DP's. My Tato's personal war began one morning as he was pushing his bicycle up a slag-heap, and another miner was riding down. They collided. My Tato's head was cracked open.

Tato put his hand to his head. When he opened his hand, blood gushed out. He fainted.

The Belgian doctors decided not to take my father to the hospital. They said, "Just leave him."

Was it a bad thing? He lay in his bed in our cozy… scary… tar-paper shack, in a coma, surrounded by people who loved him, who whispered to him that his wife and daughter were being taken care of. *(She does it in Ukrainian.)* There was the smell of cooking.

I'd pat him, and he'd look at me, but he wouldn't see me. He'd look right through me.

Three days later Tato suddenly sat bolt upright and said, "Wife, I'm hungry as a wolf. Give me breakfast!"

He was back to himself. He was fine. He was resurrected after three days. It was a miracle of God.

BANDURIST
/BASS: A-a-minnn.

> *LUBA takes an "Amen moment" (A prayer-like feeling of being in Church.)*

LUBA: But a blood clot had formed and put pressure on his brain. Soon Tato started having seizures and he stopped working in the coal mines. When we emigrated to Canada—he became lost in the medical system...I was his translator—at ten years-old, but I couldn't always be there for him. I wish I could have. There was so much I could have said for him.

Despite it all, though, Tato had an indomitable spirit! And he was double jointed.

Once when a psychiatrist in Ottawa was evaluating the extent of his brain damage from the accident, he said, "Luba, ask your father what he can do."

My father pulled up his pant leg, unjointed his knee and said, "I can do this!"

> *She demonstrates the unjointed knee and laughs at his amazing spirit, with pride. It's her spirit, too.*

> *Transition.*

In Ottawa, my Tato was sent back and forth to the mental asylum in Brockville, as an "out-patient", for "evaluation". And my mother was working as a baker in the Lord Elgin Hotel, and soon, I started going to French school.

We rented one room in a house on Charlotte Street—not far from the Russian Embassy, which my Tato kept an eye on... In the house were two French Canadian sisters, who adored me.

> *LUBA imitates both SISTERS cooing over LUBA and LUBA loving the attention.*

SISTER #1:   Ah, ma petite chou-chou...viens ici chérie!

SISTER #2:   Alors, notre petite oiseau...we will take you to the movie! Donne-moi un gros bec, minou, Luba.

YOUNG
LUBA: Merci, Madame...je veux dire, Mademoiselle.

LUBA: Living in the house with the sisters was also their grandfather, Grandpère, who was ancient and played his creaky violin all day. But only one tune.

                LUBA does the sound of the violin scratching away at the same melody ("Au clair de la lune."). LUBA imitates the violin again, and herself listening to it.

                One day, my Tato was watching through the keyhole, as usual, when he noticed a gentlemen caller—a young man—walk into the younger sister's room. Half an hour later, he walked out again, and then another man was coming up the stairs.

STEPAN: Oh my god! We're living in a whorehouse!

                We hear the sound of the scratchy violin.

LUBA: My parents decided they had to put me in a safe place. Who would look after me now that the sisters, who were entertaining gentlemen callers, could not be trusted? I was only six years old. There was no such thing as daycare or babysitters. My mother working sixteen hours a day; my Tato was being kept in Brockville for "observation".

MAMA: *(Baking.)* What to do with Luba?

LUBA: My mother was talking to this Ukrainian woman who was a cook at an orphanage run by the Grey Nuns in a ritzy mansion in Rockcliffe.

MAMA'S
FRIEND: Why don't you put Luba here?

MAMA: Will they take her? If we're not...dead?

MAMA'S
FRIEND: Sure. You can convince them, Olya.

MAMA: Yes... *(Hesitating, trying to convince herself she can do it.)* They won't say no. I don't take no.

LUBA: My Tato was an out-patient in a mental hospital, and I felt like an in-patient at the orphanage.

               I went from a whorehouse to an orphanage.

               Lighting change into opera house.

               I've played ladies of the night many times in my career. Don't be surprised. Look at me!

               Music (From the opera of Massenet's "Manon.")

               I was eighteen years old, *(LUBA sings from "Manon.")* a student at the National Theatre School of Canada, in Montreal, and the Opera, *Manon* was being presented at the Place des Arts. Here is a brief summary of the Opera: Manon, a woman of ill-repute, is sent off to the middle of nowhere, and the opera goes on and on and they put her on a boat with all these other harlots, and then she takes forever to die in the fifth act.

               The students in my class were all asked to do walk-on parts as courtesans. Well, there is no such thing as a simple walk on, for me. Or a simple courtesan.

               She struts across the stage as her whore character and sings "Loretta".

               My scarlet woman was called, "Loretta". The chorus sang out your name. "Loretta...oooo... oooo", and you'd have to go on the boat. Some of the courtesans were like, "ooh, I'm scared to go."

But Loretta was like 'Eh! Put me on the boat.'(*Does Italian up-yours finger gesture.*) And what do you know? I got a laugh.

I looked around me. I could hardly believe it. From living with loose women to playing one on the huge stage of the Place des Arts in front of 3000 people.

Lights and music restore.

As LUBA takes in the memory, and remembers something else.

(*Softly.*) ...high ceilings, beautiful moldings, stained glass windows: I walk into this grand entrance at the orphanage, with my mother. I'm six years old. It's a mansion, and to the side are these ornate carved wooden benches piled high to the ceiling with toys—dolls, teddy bears! Wonderful! However, they were not to be touched, they were the display. Non. Ne touche pas.

And then my mother left me. I watched her go, trying not to run after her. The nuns held my hands.

That evening, I remember four nuns sitting on a wooden swing with me, such a beautiful night, swinging back and forth, and back and forth with the moonlight kissing my face... The nuns peacefully, softly praying on their rosaries... They were so kind to me...

Beat.

Mama was allowed to visit once a week on Sunday from one to three. The nuns believed that if I went home on weekends, it would be harder to come back. I don't know about that...

My mother's dealing with her own immigrant fears, like: will they send us back now that Stepan is crazy? The stigma of mental illness, even in our community, it was *vsted:* shame, to have a father like mine. They called him *(In Ukrainian.) Durnuy Goy*—Crazy Goy—behind his back.

He formed a little orchestra in the mental asylum with the other inmates. Of course, he played the mandolin.

STEPAN: *(Sings.)* Oh it's Doctor Proctor, he's a little shocker, he'll fry your brain and put it in a locker.

> *Lights and music transition.*

Soon, after I arrived in the orphanage, there was a major car accident. A big, wealthy French Canadian family was involved. The mother had a two-year-old in her arms and was pregnant, and they died, like seven members of the family died. It was in all the papers. And there were still a lot of kids left. The girls who survived came to the orphanage.

I remember this nine year-old girl crumpled into a heap at the bottom of the cement stairwell—curled up weeping. Alone. Nobody was comforting her. I sat on the steps, put my arms around her, while she sobbed and sobbed.

> *YOUNG LUBA rocks the girl and comforts her. She holds her, and starts to do silly little things to make her laugh—maybe blowing the feathers off her face like with Oksana, making animal noises, somehow making the bereaved girl giggle.*
>
> *LUBA smiles, pleased with herself and inspired.*
>
> *Mozart on the Bandura. Transition.*
>
> *LUBA hears the music and stands.*

MISS
BLACKSTONE: *(A teacher. In a deep voice.)* Luba, come here a minute.

YOUNG
LUBA: Yes, Miss Blackstone…?

MISS
BLACKSTONE: I want to talk to you. No, it's not a detention.

> *LUBA walks in, teenage-like, masking her worry…*

(In a deep voice.) "Miss Barbara Blackstone" was one of *those* teachers. The one who sets you on your real life path. As opposed to the path your parents had planned for you.

(In a deep voice.) "Miss Barbara Blackstone" was my grade seven music teacher. When we walked into her classroom, she always had a record playing: Mozart, Bach, Beethoven *(duh duh duh DUH.)*.

> *LUBA, again is back to sulking in the classroom, as a teenager, worried but brash.*

Luba, I want you to try out for the public speaking contest. I'm sure you'll find something to talk about—goodness knows you have plenty to talk about in class. Talk about what is important to you.

LUBA: I'm pretty sure I'm A.D.D., so it was hard to choose one thing. Then my mind opened up: My Tato's message:

"…Good Canadian, then God then *Ukraina*!…"

Well, I focused on the part that was about me: good Canadian: hula hoops, yo-yo, hockey!

I was just about to become Canada's newest and shortest citizen. So, I decided to talk about our voyage. How I came here by boat and landed at Pier 21, a poor immigrant family with no English and no prospects and how proud I was going to be that I was going to become a Canadian citizen.

Well guess who won the contest! There was not a dry eye in the house.

I sent a limo to bring Miss Blackstone to the National Arts Centre when the Air Farce received a Governor General's Performing Arts award.

When she met my son, Gabe, she said, "Oh, there were many tears, but it was worth it."

This summer, she turns 93.

> *LUBA sings a Happy Birthday toast in Ukrainian.*

> *Transition.*

Good Canadian. Check, Tato.

STEPAN:　　Yes, but don't forget God and *Ukraina* my little messenger?

It wasn't until 1990 that I got to go to Ukraine for the first time. I was offered a part in a movie that was being filmed there. I jumped at the chance. A golden opportunity: to be in a feature film! In Ukraine! The director said the role is of the *Shynkharka*! Yes! I'll take it… What's a *Shynkharka*? Well, I was to play another lady of quality. But I was moving up in the world of women of ill-fame: I was a Madame—who fed wine, food and girls to the Cossacks in the 1800s.

At the Air Canada boarding gate, the flight attendant knew I was going to Ukraine, and he reached into his briefcase, and pulled out a simple wooden rosary.

(As the flight attendant, in a Ukrainian accent.): "Take this, Luba. It might help you."

I was touched. I thought it was bizarre, but I have a thing for rosaries, and free stuff, so I took it.

I didn't have my own rosary anymore. My mother gave it away when I was a child…

Liturgical music.

When my father died, my mother wrapped his hands with my precious mother of pearl rosary. I saw it, lying on his chest in his coffin.

YOUNG
LUBA: "Mama, that's my rosary.

MAMA: Don't you want Tato to have something of yours?

YOUNG
LUBA: *(Shakes her head, no.)*

MAMA: Luba…

               Music stops.

LUBA: Damn it, I'll take the flight attendant's rosary. And it did help me…

               It was after Chernobyl, and before the Orange Revolution. Ukraine was still communist and very Russified, which means—everyone wants to be paid under the table. I was supposed to be staying at a five star hotel. I could see five stars through the hole in my ceiling.

               Ukraina was… overwhelming. I bawled my way through Kyiv with my mother's sister, Aunt Valia, and the film's director.

               I wanted to do something meaningful on this trip, besides playing a Madame in a movie.

               There was a law that you could not paint or renovate a church *unless* lightning had struck it. Well, as luck would have it, lightning had struck this beautiful church in Kyiv! So they were able to restore it.

               My Aunt told me that this was the day when people

could leave flowers for the dead in the church. Aha! So, I bought this huge purple dahlia—a giant Chernobyl dahlia—I wanted to leave it for my father in this church—that had been resurrected by a stroke of lightning! Tato would have loved that. But the sign said that the church closed at four. It was just after four. (The number four figures in my life—it will later too, stick with me.). Anyway, Aunt Valia says:

AUNT: *Lubatchka, dorohenka.* We missed the church. Let's go eat.

LUBA: Wait, *Tsiotsa* Valia. I'm going to ask someone to open the door for us.

AUNT: *Neh Mozhlevo.*

LUBA: Of course, I can! She won't say no. I don't take no. I'll just ask.

AUNT: *Zabudsia.* Let's go.

    Music underscore.

Well, that's like a red flag to a bull. *(Singing.)* "Whatever Luba wants, Luba gets."

Then I see in the distance a little nun standing in a doorway and observing us. I thought, Yes! A nun! I love nuns! I lived with the Grey Nuns for a year in the orphanage, I can do this. I gesture to the nun—can I come and talk to you? Like a ghost, she nods.

    LUBA nods, slowly, like an apparition.

She was nineteen, with the sweetest face. I tell her I'm an actress from Canada.

I have this flower for my dead Tato. He was very religious and always loved Ukraine. Is it possible for someone to open the church?

YOUNG NUN: And the film is?

LUBA: It's, uh, it's a comedy. About a, uh, business woman.

          I didn't tell her I was playing a Madame...to show her I was religious—

          Look! I have a rosary!

          The nun sends me off to a small waiting room and says, "Stay here. I'll be right back."

          Transition into church.

          Church interior in a warm golden light.

          In the room, there is this oil painting of Christ. It is so beautiful, so touching, the expression in his eyes, what was it? Kindness? Goodness? Pity? It was so human—*(To God.)*—no offense. I start crying. I can't stop. I am standing there weeping.

          Lights and music change.

          The nun returns with the keys. She wraps my arm with both of hers, unlocks a side door, and ushers us into the church. The light, it's magic hour, there are high ceilings, art everywhere, everything is painted blue and gold. You can see the dust in the sunlight.

          Beat.

          We had heard all these stories a thousand times from our parents who went through so much. My mother watching her father die of starvation when she was nine years old during Stalin's forced famine in 1933. The *Holodomor*. People were eating grass. Millions died.

          Seeing Kyiv after Chernobyl...frescos crumbling because of the pollution and war, old women begging outside the church. People, still starving. And a little nun, holding my arm, opening doors for the luckiest comedienne in Canada.

Oh, I get it, I think: What we gained coming to Canada. And what they lost.

I open my wallet and pull out a twenty dollar U.S. bill to hand it to the young nun with all this goodness in her. She jumps back like I had shown her poison or the devil himself. And then she points to a collection box. I put the twenty in there.

(A moment of prayer in Ukrainian for Tato.) Spochuvaij z Bohom, Tato.

> *She takes a deep breath, mimes smelling the huge flower and smiles as she puts it down for Tato. Does a small salute pre-echoing the end of the play.*

BANDURIST
/BASS: *(Sings.)* AAMIN…

> *Lights change.*

LUBA: I used to pray all the time—that my Tato would get better. But he didn't.

Prayer did work for me, though, when I lost Pretty Peter.

My budgie, my best friend, my soul mate! He was an escape artist, the little green bastard. One day he got out. He flew like a drunken little airplane, flitting back and forth. Gone!

My Tato had died that January, when I was twelve years old, and now I lost Peter, so my life was over. That was the end of it. I prayed with all my being.

YOUNG
LUBA: "Please. Please dear God, get me Peter. He's going to die out there… I promise I will be so good. I

know it's my fault he flew away! But, he's so little, and scared and he's so alone...he's all I have...I'll be good! I'll study hard, and help Mama, I promise! Just watch Peter for me...keep him safe dear Lord, I am praying for this. I thank you for hearing me."

LUBA: My teacher, Miss Evelyn Clarke, knew how much I was suffering with the loss of my father. Unbeknownst to me, she sent an all-out bulletin to the public schools in the area to look out for Pretty Peter.

A couple of months later, Miss Clarke told me to sit down.

MISS
CLARKE: "Luba, a green budgie flew into a Grade Two class."

YOUNG
LUBA: It's pretty Peter!

LUBA: Yes, it was him, the bad, bad boy. Thank you, Jesus!

He flew away again about a year later. This time I didn't pray. I knew I'd be pushing it.

Transition into ghost story.

You're going to think this is weird... I do too, believe me, but, you know, we're friends now, so we can talk. Well, I can talk...We were doing the Air Farce, in the early TV days, and a waiter in a restaurant asked for my autograph for his wife. I noticed he was really agitated. Yes, yes, I have that effect on people. He told me that his wife, Julie, had Non-Hodgkin's lymphoma. She was diagnosed on her 40th birthday. She was forty-two and had lost her hair twice. They had three children. Of course, I gave him the autograph!

Then, as usual, I meddle into other people's lives.

LUBA: I'd like to make Julie some Esiak tea, it's a very healing native tea.

The husband was like, "hmmm… Okay."

That night, I was compelled to pray.

Not in the way you do every day.

You know, not like 'dear sweet Jesus, just take me! Take me to your home so I don't have to do this Easter Egg Ukrainian Festival! Why, why, why did I say yes? I'm not prepared… I'm late, always late!' And then the audience is laughing and I come offstage and I'm like, 'Thank you, Jesus! Don't take me now! Just remind me next time to say 'no.'

At the time, I had five cats. I'm down to four now, okay, so I'm not a crazy old cat lady. They usually sleep on my bed.

Praying for Julie so exhausted me, I threw my cats out of the room. And they were like "Mom!"… (*She does an imitation of the cats, annoyed and giving her the finger and skulking away.*)

> *Lights and music change.*

> *She's using a shawl like a blanket, under which she's sleeping on the bench.*

4:44 a.m. Standing at the foot of the bed is this apparition. (*She hides under the blanket and peeks out to say:*) I told you this was weird, just stay with me. It's a tall native woman with white hair in a bun, I could see the detail of beading on her dress. She was very old, but had no wrinkles.

Eeeee. I'm paralyzed, but fascinated. What the hell is this now? I used to play all these psychics, so I was used to making fun of it. (*As the psychic.*)

Madame Zostroska sees everything…ah yes, there will be an election next year…

The apparition is very close. She bows. *(LUBA gets up and nods and bows, slowly, reminiscent of the young nun in Ukraine.)* It takes fifteen seconds. Then she just disintegrates. I turn on the light.

Lights restore.

4:44 a.m. and she was gone. And I had to pee so badly.

'Hello, um, ghost, if you're still here, could you please move because I have to pee.'

I opened the bedroom door and all the cats are right there. Sitting up. Not sleeping. All gathered on top of the stairs, looking at me.

'Hi, come in kitties! Come to mommy! Up onto the bed! That's right. Under the covers, please!'

So, the next day, I make the native Esiak tea. Julie, this woman I've never met who has cancer, is going for dinner with me and my friend, Linda, who is Chinese. And you know that in Chinese numerology, the number 4 is death, 44 is double death, and I saw the old Native woman at 4:44 *(To the audience.)*. See? The number 4 again. Isn't that satisfying? The way I've come back to it, like I said I would, earlier in the show?

BANDURIST plays a "reminder" chord. LUBA gets back on track.

Right, so, we take Julie to a restaurant. Julie tells me that her great-grandmother was full-blooded Ojibway.

LUBA: What did she look like? You see, last night, I saw this…this…apparition. Or maybe it was a—

Linda cuts me off.

LINDA: It wasn't a dream. What time did she come?

LUBA: Oh I don't know, just before dawn.

I don't want to jinx this whole thing with the 444.

Julie didn't want to die, and I did not want to stir up the shit, so I lied. "Oh around dawn..."

Then, I find out that according to native spirituality, 4 is the best time for a spirit to come—4 corners, 4 elements, 4 seasons. An excellent time.

A few months later Julie called me, "Well, the pathologist said, 'I don't know what you've been doing but the tumours are gone, you're cancer free.'"

Yes! Was it the tea? The prayer? The apparition? The cats? The chemo? Luck? Who cares? Julie is a grandmother now.

(Ukrainian toast.) Dhai Bhozheh Zdorovia!

And so am I! (She toasts herself.) Baba Luba!

Isn't that weird? How suddenly you're a grandmother! I still feel like that sexy fifteen year-old, just busting away from her parents, moonlighting at a little café in Ottawa.

Lights and music transition into 1960s coffee house.

1960s folk music in the Ottawa coffee house, Le Hibou—Gordon Lightfoot, played by the BANDURIST— "Early morning rain..."

LUBA grooves sexily to the music and sings some Gordon Lightfoot.

All through my high-school years, I worked at Le

Hibou Coffee House on Sussex Drive. It was an incredible space. And it was my chance to escape. Yes! Freedom. No more accordion, *Vinoks*, red boots! No more *Ukrainaznavstvo* studies! Enough! Time for some jazz! Time for theatre! It was the generation of go-go boots, short skirts, love beads, poetry. Le Hibou!

Bruce Cockburn played. I served him coffee.

Dave Broadfoot did standup. Served him coffee.

Buffy Sainte-Marie, *(In a Buffy voice.)* "Some coffee, Buffy?"

Gordon Lightfoot.

YOUNG
LUBA: *(Seductively, and awkwardly like a fifteen year old.)* Coffee, Gordie?

LUBA: And I thought, 'I want to be a part of that!'

               But how...?

               Lights and music (Stratford Festival fanfare). Transition:

               And, I ended up at the National Theatre School and, I got to audition for the Stratford Festival with my graduating class! After doing my mandatory two classical audition pieces, I thought to myself, okay, how am I going to stand out here?

DIRECTOR: Miss Goy, thank you for the Strindberg, thank you for the Shakespeare.

LUBA: Wait! Please, sir, Mr. Gascon, I, I just have one more small piece I'd like to perform.

DIRECTOR: Well, I'm sorry, you're out of—

               Abrupt light change:

LUBA interrupts and does the whole monologue. It's a caustic piece where she plays a six year-old girl, Angela:

YOUNG
LUBA:

"So, I was standing on the corner waiting for someone to cross me, cuz I'm not allowed to cross the street by myself, and this Lady comes along and says ..."Here is a bubble gum sample, do you chew this brand?"...And I say..."I don't like bubble gum". So the Lady takes out a pad and pencil, and she writes that down. Then she says..."Why don't you like it? Is it the design of the wrapper? And I say, "No-o-o...it's cuz I can't blow bubbles."....So she writes that down. And then she says..." How would you like a bubble gum which is guaranteed to blow bubbles? ...And I said... "I don't know... I'm not allowed to cross the street by myself. And I'm not allowed to watch what I want to watch... and my father keeps calling me by my older sister's name! And everything's always my fault! It's me... Always me! ...And all of a sudden I'm crying, and yelling. So then a crowd comes along...and some Big Guy says... "Is this Lady bothering you girlie?" And the crowd turns ugly. So the Lady gets very nervous...she drops her pad and pencil in the street, and she's asking everybody... "Why don't you like it!? Is it the design of the wrapper? And nobody knows what she's talking about! ... So then...I went home."

DIRECTOR: Luba, excellent audition, I would like to hire you for the Stratford company.

YOUNG
LUBA:　　　Really?

DIRECTOR: Mais, oui.

YOUNG
LUBA:

How would I fit in, where would you put me? I'm

not pretty enough for Juliet and too young for the nurse.

DIRECTOR: We'll find a way.

YOUNG
LUBA: Thank you very much but I'll believe it when I see the contract.

DIRECTOR: I'm serious.

YOUNG
LUBA: So am I.

    Exits with excitement.

    Light change.

LUBA: And they did. They hired me for two seasons. I didn't really fit into Stratford, though.

Surprised?

Soon after, another director suggested I audition for this sketch troupe in Toronto, *The Jest Society.* After Pierre Trudeau's "We will have a just society." They did political satire. Which was explained to me as, "comforting the afflicted and afflicting the comfortable."

I asked the director, 'Political satire? I'm an actress! Do I have to listen to CBC radio and read *The Globe and Mail*?'

DIRECTOR: Luba, that would be helpful.

LUBA: They hired me anyway.

I was enchanted by these guys. They cared so much about what was happening to us Canadians. But, what could I talk about? What do I say?

Well... Pierre Trudeau was dating Barbra Streisand. Boy was that a gift.

Sings the song: "People."

People really thought I was Barbra Streisand—can I have your autograph? And I'd give it to them. As Barbra *(She does it.)*.

Next, we went to pitch a political satire show to CBC radio. It was 1973. The boys were on their way to register the name for our radio show. It was to be called *"The Beaver Follies"*. In the car, on the radio, they heard former Prime Minister John Deifenbaker on a rampage about...

(As Diefenbaker.): "They're taking the Royal Canadian out of everything. Royal instant pudding, it's gonna be instant pudding."

One of the guys said, "Hey, we could be the *Royal Canadian Air Farce*". And you know, if we'd been *"The Beaver Follies"* we never would have lasted 35 years.

Who knew when I started improvising that I'd end up improvising with the whole country?

We were in Winnipeg, one of Canada's Ukie Capitals. And I'd never done Ukrainian on the radio. All this time, I had tried to get away from my past, SO HARD. Melding these two worlds really made me nervous, I mean this Ukrainian shtick wasn't me anymore, was it? But, still, I had this great character I was dying to do...

We did a sketch with John Morgan as a dowager with her own radio show.

> *LUBA does herself as a Ukrainian farm woman calling in talking about her budgie bird and her husband and her pantyhose.*

JOHN: Hello...Amy Della Pommpa here....you're on the air...go ahead next caller.

LUBA: (*As a Ukrainian farm woman.*) *Hallo Amychka... Vitaemo Vas do Vinnipegoo! Yah majiou problemyh iz moim 'budgie bird'! Toi malenkuy 'pecker'r' yist moji panty-hose! Shcho ya mayo robuteh? Help me.*

There was a laugh, then a pause, as John replies:

JOHN: "How nice to hear from our French Canadian friends..."

Well, when the Ukrainians heard this, the entire Ukrainian nation of Canada adopted me. They insisted I was from Winnipeg... So be it.

BABA
SAFRONIA: "Ah, Luba, we be see you on the television."

LUBA: I do a radio show.

BABA
SAFRONIA: We be see you on the radio too. Here, Luba, I make dis for you. A purse...

Yeah, I be Baba Safronia, everybody call me Baba. Whether we be Anglophone or Francophone or Ukophone, or got no phone at all, we're all the same under the skin, we have no clothes on.

It was great to be the only woman in the cast. Mind you, the boys would never lend me their pantyhose. But I got to play everybody:

She does a quick montage of her favourite characters:

HANNAH
GARTNER: (*Former host of CBC's Fifth Estate.*) Hullo...I'm Hannah Gartner, and my hands need Valium.

BRENDA the
BINGO LADY: Do you see the television now, five hundred channels? Men spend more time on the couch in front of the television with the remote control than

in bed with their spouses. I say, keep those channels coming.

PRESTON
MANNING: Hi, I'm Preston Manning, Leader of the Refoooorm party.

MARGARET
ATWOOD: I'm Margaret Atwood, and I'm so excited to be here. I'm about to lose control, and I think I like it.

SHEILA
COPPS: *(Yelling.)* I could have been the Prime Minister of Canada! Do you hear me! Prime Minister Sheila... PMS!

I loved Anne Murray—who came on our show and I tried to get her to sing *Snowbird*. I was playing the Queen:

ANNE: No.

THE QUEEN: Oh, come on Anne, dadaddada...

ANNE: No!

She swore she'd never sing *Snowbird* again, even for the Queen.

THE QUEEN: —hm hm hm...

Oh, sometimes being on TV is very glamorous.

We did this sketch—we'd heard the Queen had rodent problems in Buckingham Palace, so we used live mice on the set. They placed one on my shoulder, while I, as the Queen, was like, 'Hello. Yes, Philip and I are having a small rodent problem." Dozens of mice are running all over my desk. I was supposed to pick one up by the tail. Well, have you ever tried to pick up a mouse by a tail? I went for the tail... It's gone! It's gone somewhere on my body! Where is it?

During notes, the Director asks, "Luba, could you just pick up that mouse a little faster?" Yeah right, glamorous.

I got to meet her Majesty the Queen. She and Prince Philip were unveiling this horrible statue at CBC. I can't remember anything about her Majesty except this little gloved hand coming out, "Helloo". And I'm just trying not to *(As the Queen.)* "Helloooo". Sheila Copps was right beside me, and I said to her Majesty, "I impersonate politicians. I do Ms. Copps."

SHEILA: But you're not doing me nowwww.

LUBA: Once you meet the politicians—it's harder to make fun of them, but you have to—everyone needs to be taken down a notch or two, don't you think?

In the last years, we brought in the young people because in High Def television, you can see everything. We couldn't play all those characters anymore. On radio, I'll always be tall and young and have a body like Angelina Jolie...

Our pact was we'd keep doing it as long as we were having fun. For John Morgan, television wasn't fun, so he got out. For me, it was still fun even until the end. We'd always end up laughing, even when we had our disagreements. Laughter sustained us.

People I meet on the streets are so comfortable with me now, after going into their living rooms all these years. They're like family. They talk to me, invite me to things. ...Sure! I'll say yes to anything! You never know who you'll meet.

Lights and music.

In 2009, I got a phone call with the letters GDC on the phone display:

'Gabe, hang up it's some telemarketer."

No,—it was 'Government du Canada'. It was Governor General Michaëlle Jean's office: *(With a French accent.)* "Would you be available, Ms. Goy, to come to a State Dinner for Ukrainian President Viktor Yushchenko?"

'Let me check my calend— Do I want to meet the man who broke the grip of Moscow through the Orange Revolution and united and liberated all the Ukies after thousands of years being chained to Soviet rule?— Yes, yes, I'm available!'

In the back of the taxi, I look out the window, and all along Sussex Drive, the lampposts have the Ukrainian flag and the Canadian flag for miles and miles– all the way to Rideau Hall.

I wish Tato could have been here beside me. "Look out the window, Tato! Ukrainian flag, Canadian Flag! Ukrainian flag, Canadian Flag! Ukrainian flag, Canadian Flag! Tato!"

Oh, it was unimaginable!

Lights and music transition.

My Tato was a secret. Mama tried to shelter me, to allow me to be a child. But I knew some of the story. It wasn't until later that I learned the truth...or at least, the facts...

My Tato suffered from depression. Because he couldn't work! He wasn't crazy, he was sick! *(She does a quick recall of the plotting cohorts, they say, "Crazy Goy.")* They were sending him back and forth to the wrong place...

All he wanted was to come home for Ukrainian Christmas on January 6th. His doctor told him they were going to do a lobotomy on him in February.

He'd either be a vegetable or it would fix it for good. My Tato said, "I need to go home for Christmas and see my family." They said, "It's January. Christmas is over." They made him feel like an idiot. What could he do...?

Ukrainian Christmas Carol: LUBA and BASS sing one verse together and then BASS continues under...

LUBA: It was Ukrainian Christmas. Time for family, carols, church, delicious *holobtsi, kapusnyiak,* honey cookies and tables covered with the finest of embroidery. Mama insisted we put fresh sheets on the beds before we went to dinner at my Godmother's house.

The doorbell rings, loud. *Brriiing* I run downstairs. There was a telegram! Cool. We didn't have a phone. The messenger said, sign here.

LUBA opens and reads the telegram.

"We regret to inform you that your husband Stepan Goy died at 2:45 a.m."

We couldn't comprehend what it meant.

YOUNG
LUBA: *(Reading the telegram.)* "We regret to inform you..."

I grabbed my coat and ran downstairs. My mother was screaming after me:

MAMA: *(In Ukrainian.)* Luba! Luba! Where are you going?

YOUNG
LUBA: I have to go.

MAMA: *Dorohenkah.* Don't leave me!

YOUNG
LUBA: I'll be back. I'll find someone to help us!

MAMA: *(In Ukrainian.)* Don't leave me!

YOUNG
LUBA: I'll come back, Mama!

LUBA: I ran out into this cold night. Running, down the
               hill, running, down the street. Calling: "Tato! Tato!
               Tato!" Running, my lungs bursting. I end up at
               these friends of my parents, these twin sisters and
               their husbands. "Tato! Tato's dead!" They had a car
               and a phone, so maybe they could help.

                    Music/carol stops.

               I draw a blank after that.

                    Transition into Rideau Hall.

               The State Dinner was packed with Canadian
               Ukrainian literati. All the singers, artists, and
               filmmakers. The Director of Opera from Kyiv, a
               very pompous man, sat at my table.

DIRECTOR
OF OPERA: *(In Ukrainian.) Ya Direktor Opera z Kyiva!*

LUBA: I was in an opera once… *(Sings.) Loretta…*

               Her Excellency Michaëlle Jean is doing a speech.
               She mentions my name. *(LUBA reacts.)* People start
               to clap. I'm thinking, "Do you mind, she's making a
               speech." Elated and embarrassed at the same time,
               I stand up. Tempting as it is to do some shtick—a
               little Queen wave or something—No. It's serious.

               All of a sudden, during the dinner, someone
               whispers, "The President of Ukraine is coming
               to our table!" I put my perogie-stuffed lambchop
               away! I'm thinking: should I call him Mr. President
               or Mr. Yushchenko or President Yushchenko? He
               knows he's the President, what do I say…?

                    *Lights and music (Ukrainian, liturgical.) transition
                    to Tato.*

I could hear the whispers. At my Tato's funeral. Two weeks later, I confronted Mama.

YOUNG
LUBA:

"Mama, what is going on? What are you hiding from me? I want the truth."

LUBA:

She had her back to me. She straightened up, took a breath, looked at me and said: "Well, your father hung himself."

YOUNG
LUBA:

"He *what*? That's not true. Tato loved life. He loved people, and music, and poetry. He loved us—how could he do that and not tell me?"

LUBA:

So many times over the years, I thought: I will go back to that place: 'What did you do to him that he should have to hang himself on Ukrainian Christmas? A young man, 36 years old, with a little girl and a wife that he loved—the surgery was supposed to be in February, a month later—just let him go home to sing in the choir!'

But I never did go back. I never <u>said</u> anything.

Lights and music return to State Dinner.

(As someone at the table whispering nervously to her.) "The President of Ukraine is standing right behind you…Luba!"

I stand, turn around, and look up. He's six foot four inches.

I'm looking at his armpit.

I'm speechless. Waiting for him to say something.

He doesn't say anything. He just looks down at me. Kind, kind eyes, but expectant.

And we're standing there. Looking at each other. In silence.

I think: I have to say something—everyone who is dead now—who suffered and made art and poetry and music and prayer and bread and life—would kill me if I didn't say something to the President of free Ukraine! I'm just a DP comedienne what am I going to say? I could feel this bubble in my chest, rising up, ready to burst... In pure Ukrainian I say, "Paneh Yushchenko, from the bottom of my heart, I want to thank you so much for what you have done to free Ukraine. My Tato, Stepan Goy, was a colossal patriot. He died when I was twelve. His biggest dream was to see freedom and democracy in Ukraine, which you have attained. He would be so proud of you, which we all are. I want to thank you."

Yushchenko looks at me, and I feel his warmth... But he doesn't say anything to me.

Lights change. The chandelier glows red light on.

The parish priest didn't want to bury my father in the Ukrainian cemetery because he'd committed suicide. A man whose whole life was about: "Good Canadian, God and *Ukraina*". Not good enough to be buried in hallowed ground?

There was one good man, a priest, Father Paszicney, who said:

FATHER
PASZICNEY: 'I will bury him. I know Stepan to be a religious, good, loving man. He suffered. He was in pain.'

LUBA: Father Paszicney had actually traveled to the mental hospital to see Tato just before he died. Tato had requested a Priest: "I want my last rites. I'm going to die." Why did he say that?

They buried him, thanks to one good man.

Lights and music change. Camera flash, back to State Dinner.

The President of Ukraine bends down, scoops me up, and presses his cheek against mine, and holds me so hard. Then he steps back and looks at me, with such goodness in his eyes. I think, "My father would die if he wasn't already dead." Then I think, 'if this President is hitting on me—oh boy'.

She inhales his smell.

You know how you smell aftershave or soap on someone? The President's white shirt smelled like fresh air—just clean. Like the wind over the meadows in Belgium, the empty Church in Kyiv, my grandbaby's fuzzy head, the sun on fresh linen, He smelled good.

I pull out the camera and say, 'Can I have a picture of you and me?'

He puts his arm around my shoulder.

Lights change.

It wasn't until I saw the picture on my son's computer.

Oh my god! Look where my hand is. I have my hand on the President's cummberbund like, "He's mine girls."

Very inappropriate I guess but...I'm with the President, hello! I tell everybody, "Viktor and I, we're like this."

And then Yushchenko finally did it. He locked eyes with me, and very slowly, like an apparition, he nodded *(She nods slowly.).* As if to say, I got the message, Luba. How important freedom was to me, and is to all of us. How the past matters long after it's too late to change it. How your history will never let you go until you, and sometimes your whole nation, free yourself from it. How your life is not a squirrel in a blue bin, or a lost budgie or an opera, but a mission that, even if someone else has sent you on it, you have to finish.

She finishes her nod.

The circle is completed.

That's it, Tato. I've done my bit. Message delivered. And received.

Slowly, taking fifteen seconds, she bows. As lights get brighter and brighter and brighter and then black out.

The End.